Understanding the Surge in Global Heat Records: Unraveling the Causes Behind Earth's Warming Trend

Introduction:

The Earth is experiencing an unprecedented surge in heat records, with the past two years witnessing alarming spikes in temperature.

This phenomenon has sparked widespread concern among scientists, policymakers, and the public alike, as it signifies the intensification of global warming and its potentially catastrophic consequences.

In this book, we delve into the multifaceted reasons behind the Earth's breaking heat records, exploring the interplay of natural variability and human-induced climate change.

Human-Induced Climate Change

At the forefront of the escalating heat records lies human-induced climate change.

The combustion of fossil fuels, deforestation, industrial processes, and other anthropogenic activities have significantly elevated atmospheric concentrations of greenhouse gases, such as carbon dioxide (CO_2), methane (CH_4), and nitrous oxide (N_2O).

These gases trap heat within the Earth's atmosphere, creating a greenhouse effect that warms the planet.

The relentless increase in greenhouse gas emissions over the past century has accelerated this warming trend, leading to the disruption of global climate patterns.

<u>Widespread Deforestation and Land Use Changes</u>

Deforestation and land use changes have also played a pivotal role in exacerbating global warming.

Forests act as carbon sinks, absorbing CO2 from the atmosphere through the process of photosynthesis.

However, widespread deforestation, primarily driven by agricultural expansion, logging, and urbanization, has significantly reduced the Earth's natural capacity to sequester carbon.

This loss of carbon sinks has contributed to the buildup of greenhouse gases in the atmosphere, amplifying the greenhouse effect and leading to higher temperatures worldwide.

Feedback Mechanisms and Tipping Points

Another critical factor driving the surge in heat records is the activation of feedback mechanisms and tipping points within the Earth's climate system.

As temperatures rise, various feedback loops come into play, further amplifying warming.

For instance, the melting of polar ice caps and glaciers reduces the Earth's albedo, or its ability to reflect sunlight, leading to increased absorption of solar radiation and further warming.

Similarly, the thawing of permafrost releases large quantities of methane, a potent greenhouse gas, into the atmosphere, intensifying the greenhouse effect.

Natural Variability and Extreme Weather Events

 While human-induced climate change is the primary driver of the Earth's warming trend, natural variability also contributes to the surge in heat records.

 Natural phenomena such as El Niño and La Niña events, volcanic eruptions, and solar cycles can influence global temperatures on shorter timescales.

El Niño, for example, is associated with warmer-than-average sea surface temperatures in the equatorial Pacific Ocean, leading to widespread impacts on weather patterns and climate worldwide.

These natural variability factors can interact with anthropogenic climate change, exacerbating the frequency and intensity of extreme weather events, including heatwaves, droughts, and wildfires.

Urbanization and the Urban Heat Island Effect

The rapid expansion of urban areas has also exacerbated local and regional heat extremes through the urban heat island (UHI) effect.

Urbanization replaces natural vegetation and permeable surfaces with heat-absorbing materials such as concrete and asphalt, altering local microclimates and trapping heat.

   As a result, urban areas tend to be several degrees warmer than their surrounding rural areas, leading to increased energy consumption for cooling, heat-related health risks, and heightened temperatures during heatwaves.

Mitigation and Adaptation Strategies

Addressing the surge in global heat records requires concerted efforts to mitigate greenhouse gas emissions and adapt to the changing climate.

Transitioning to renewable energy sources, enhancing energy efficiency, promoting sustainable land-use practices, and investing in climate-resilient infrastructure are crucial steps toward mitigating climate change and reducing the frequency of extreme heat events.

Additionally, fostering international cooperation, advancing climate research and monitoring, and implementing adaptive measures at local, national, and global levels are essential for building resilience and safeguarding communities against the impacts of a warming climate.

Conclusion:

The surge in global heat records over the past two years underscores the urgent need for collective action to address climate change and its far-reaching consequences.

 While human-induced factors such as greenhouse gas emissions and land-use changes remain the primary drivers of the Earth's warming trend, natural variability and feedback mechanisms further amplify the intensity and frequency of extreme heat events.

Mitigation efforts must be coupled with adaptation strategies to build resilience and mitigate the impacts of a changing climate on ecosystems, economies, and societies worldwide.

Only through collaborative and decisive action can we hope to mitigate the worst impacts of climate change and secure a sustainable future for generations to come.

Please use the next few pages for
your notes and debates.